MASTE

Road Traffic

Series 1 Edition 1

MASTERCLASS

Q & A Study Guide for Police Exams

MASTERCLASS PASS Questions

Road Traffic

Series 1 Edition 1

Written by

Fraser Sampson and Glenn Hutton

Detail Technologies Limited

Published by

Detail Technologies Limited

Masterclass Pass Questions - Q&A Study Guide for Police Exams
ROAD TRAFFIC - Series 1 Edition 1
Fraser Sampson and Glenn Hutton

Detail Technologies Limited

Detail Technologies Limited
PO Box 43, Porth, CF39 8WR.

British Library Cataloguing in Publication Data
Data available

ISBN 0-9546129-4-9

Designed and typeset by **Splash Design**,
Bridgefield House, Bedwas, Caerphilly, CF83 8DZ
Printed in Great Britain by **Zenith Media**,
Moy Road Ind. Est., Taffs Well, Cardiff

Contents

Detail Technologies Ltd

Detail Technologies Limited has provided technology based learning aids for police officers for several years. Founded by serving police officers who understand entirely the learning process for the National Police Examinations, the company is dedicated to providing exctiting new ways to make studying easier. In addition to the IT products PASS, Quick Questions and Masterclass Questions, the new Masterclass Audio is available on CD for use in the car or away from your computer.

The award winning PASS Part 1 Question Generation Engine is now available to use via the Detail web site. PASS ONLINE™ provides several features found in PASS via a web server. Log on via the website at www.detail-technologies.co.uk and sign up for a free trial. View the 2004 Blackstone Manuals on-line whilst you are studying. Take an on-line examination. Access a trainer who will be able to answer your legal query or partake in discussions via the on-line legal bulletin board.

Quick Questions Mobile allows you to receive questions by textphone. Text EXAM to 88199 and you will be sent a question by return. Send your answer and you will be told whether you are correct or wrong.

All Detail products are designed to enhance your chances of exam success. For further information telephone 0870 800 2 999 or check out www.detail-technologies.co.uk.

The Authors

Fraser Sampson LL.B., LL.M., MBA Solicitor

Formerly the Head of National Police Training Examinations & Assessment, Fraser Sampson has considerable experience in the strategic and operational management of assessment, selection, recruitment processes and professional qualifying examinations. While working for the Home Office, Fraser provided advice to the Police Promotion Examinations Board and several advisory groups. Having published many articles across a range of professional journals, Fraser is the author of several current professional texts including the best-selling Blackstone's Police Manuals (published by Oxford University Press). Fraser is now a qualified solicitor practising at the award winning national law firm, Walker Morris, where he specialises in Employment and Police work. Fraser can be contacted at fis@walkermorris.co.uk.

Glenn Hutton BA., M.Phil., FCIPD

Glenn Hutton is co-author of the Blackstone Police Manual Evidence and Procedure. He was formerly Head of Examinations and Assessment and Quality Assurance for National Police Training (now Centrex), Head of Training in North Yorkshire Police and worked as a Course Director and Director of Studies at the Police Staff College, Bramshill.

Glenn currently works as a private consultant to organisations concerned with recruitment and selection by way of assessment and examination and is the author of three educational text books on key skills examinations.

SERGEANTS

Road Traffic

Question RT/PS/1

Which of the following vehicles will NOT be treated as a motor vehicle as specified in s. 189 of the Road Traffic Act 1988?

A Motor vehicles being towed by another vehicle.

B Petrol-driven micro scooters.

C Pedestrian controlled vehicles.

D Electrically powered vehicles.

Answer RT/PS/1

C is correct.

Section 189 of the Road Traffic Act 1988 specifies which vehicles will not be treated as motor vehicles; they include pedestrian controlled vehicles and some implements for cutting grass.

Question RT/PS/2

Where a person's movements are beyond their control or their actions are brought about involuntarily, they will not generally be liable at criminal law as the element of actus reus is not present. A notable example of this is automatism.

In which of the following circumstances would the defence of automatism generally be available?

A A medically diagnosed diabetic continues to drive whilst experiencing the start of a hypoglycaemic episode.

B A driver suffers from reduced awareness brought on by the continuous focusing on a long, featureless road, sometimes called 'motorway hypnosis'.

C Where a swarm of bees suddenly flies into a car you are driving through an open window, causing you to collide with an oncoming vehicle.

D A driver responds to a mobile phone ringing automatically, causing the vehicle to collide with a road sign.

Answer RT/PS/2

C is correct.

Automatism might be brought about by a swarm of bees flying in through the window of a moving car or the driver lapsing into a coma (Hill v Baxter [1958] 1 All ER 193).

Question RT/PS/3

At 2am on Monday 2nd October Ahmed is involved in a road accident. He drives his car out of a junction controlled by a 'Give Way' sign into the path of an oncoming vehicle. The driver of the oncoming vehicle is killed instantly. Ahmed was on his way home from a nightclub where he had been drinking heavily.

In relation to s. 3A of the Road Traffic Act 1988, (causing death by careless driving when under the influence of drink or drugs), up to what time can Ahmed be required to provide a specimen for analysis where failure to provide, without reasonable excuse, would render him guilty of an offence?

A 6am Monday 2nd October.

B 2pm Monday 2nd October.

C 8pm Monday 2nd October.

D 2am Tuesday 3rd October.

Answer RT/PS/3

C is correct.

8pm Monday 2nd October. Section 3A of the Road Traffic Act 1988 states:

(1) If a person causes the death of another person by driving a mechanically propelled vehicle on a road or other public place without due care and attention, or without reasonable consideration for other persons using the road or place, and-
(a) he is, at the time when he is driving, unfit to drive through drink or drugs, or
(b) he has consumed so much alcohol that the proportion of it in his breath, blood or urine at that time exceeds the prescribed limit, or
(c) he is, within 18 hours after that time, required to provide a specimen in pursuance of section 7 of this Act, but without reasonable excuse fails to provide it, he is guilty of an offence.

Question RT/PS/4

The Highway Code provides one way of illustrating the standard of driving expected of a prudent and competent driver.

In which of the following circumstances has the Highway Code NOT supported the liability of a person in criminal proceedings?

A The use of mobile phones.

B Braking distances in proving speeding cases.

C The use of in-car communications equipment.

D Proceedings in relation to public passenger vehicles.

Answer RT/PS/4

B is correct.

The braking distances shown in the Highway Code are not admissible in proving speeding cases as they amount to hearsay (R v Chadwick [1975] Crim LR 105.

Question RT/PS/5

The police are investigating a road accident where one of the vehicles failed to stop. In accordance with s. 172 of the Road Traffic Act 1988 they make a request in writing and serve it by post to the keeper of the vehicle that failed to stop.

How long does the keeper have to provide the information as to the identity of the driver at the time of the accident, beginning with the day on which the requirement is served?

A 7 days.

B 14 days.

C 21 days.

D 28 days.

Answer RT/PS/5

D is correct.

Section 172(7)(a) of the Road Traffic Act 1988 provides that where the requirement is made in writing and served by post, it shall have effect as a requirement to provide the information within 28 days beginning with the day on which it is served.

Question RT/PS/6

Cawthorn parks her vehicle on a road. She sets the handbrake and turns off the ignition before alighting from the vehicle to visit a nearby post office. Vascall is sat in the front passenger seat of the vehicle and remains in the vehicle while Cawthorn visits the post office. Vascall inadvertently releases the handbrake of the vehicle that then rolls forward down a hill, eventually colliding with a parked vehicle causing considerable damage to both vehicles.

In relation to the requirements of s. 170 of the Road Traffic Act 1988 whose duty is it to stop and give their name and address or report the accident to the police?

A Cawthorne only.

B Vascall only.

C Both.

D Neither.

Answer RT/PS/6

A is correct.

Section 170 of the Road Traffic Act states:

(1) This section applies in a case where, owing to the presence of a mechanically propelled vehicle on a road or other public place, an accident occurs by which-
(a) ....
(b) damage is caused-
(i) to a vehicle other than that mechanically propelled vehicle ......
(2) The driver of the mechanically propelled vehicle must stop and, if required to do so by any person having reasonable grounds for so requiring, give his name and address ....

Where a passenger may have been directly responsible for the accident (by letting off the handbrake) , it was held that the circumstances met the requirements of s. 170 and that the driver attracted the relevant statutory duties (Cawthorne v DPP [2000] RTR 45).

Question RT/PS/7

At 10am on Monday 2nd October, Chan drives into a town and finds a place to park on the main street. However, on manoeuvring his car into the space he collides with another vehicle causing damage to its headlamp and front offside wing. There is no one with the damaged vehicle and no one returns to it even though Chan waits a reasonable length of time.

Chan has to catch a train at 12.30pm to London to attend an evening meeting and then stays overnight before returning home the following morning. At 11.30am on Tuesday 3rd October, on his way home from the railway station, Chan calls into your police station to report the accident.

Has Chan complied with the requirements of s. 170 of the Road Traffic Act 1988 in relation to his duty to report the accident?

A Yes, Chan has reported the accident as soon as reasonably practicable after the accident.

B No, Chan is required to report the accident as soon as reasonably practicable and in any case within 24 hours.

C Yes, even though Chan has not reported the accident within 24 hours he has done so as soon as reasonably practicable after that time.

D No, Chan had 24 hours in which to report the accident and failed to do so.

Answer RT/PS/7

B is correct

Section 170 of the Road Traffic Act 1988 states:

(3) If for any reason the driver of a mechanically propelled vehicle does not give his name and address under subsection (2) above, he must report the accident.
(4). . .
(5) . . .
(6)To comply with a duty under this section to report an accident ….. , the driver-
(a) . . .
(b) must do so as soon as reasonably practicable and, in any case, within twenty-four hours of the occurrence of the accident.

Question RT/PS/8

Robertson has been seen by police officers overtaking another vehicle on a pedestrian crossing and driving in a manner where they suspect he may have consumed alcohol. They cause Robertson's vehicle to stop and require him to provide a sample of breath in accordance with s. 6 of the Road Traffic Act 1988. The breath sample is negative. On talking to the officers further they notice that he is still slurring his words and arrest him under s. 4 of the 1988 Act, for being unfit through drink or drugs.

In these circumstances has Robertson been unlawfully arrested?

A Yes, Robertson has already supplied a specimen of breath which proved to be negative.

B No, if the police have reasonable cause to suspect that Robertson was impaired.

C Yes, Robertson could not be suspected of being impaired where a negative breath test has already been administered.

D No, if the evidential sample of breath taken at the police station is over the prescribed limit.

Answer RT/PS/8

B is correct.

In DPP v Robertson (2002) The Times 13 March, officers embarked on the procedure under s. 6 and breathalysed the defendant who produced a negative result. On talking to the officers further, the defendant slurred his speech when giving the name of his solicitor. The officers then arrested him under s. 4 and took him to a police station where he provided an evidential sample of breath which was over the prescribed limit. It was held that the law clearly gave a constable a power to arrest if what s/he had witnessed amounted to reasonable cause to suspect that the person was impaired.

Question RT/PS/9

Billingham is involved in an accident where his car leaves the road on a bend and collides with a stone wall. Damage is caused to the car but the stone wall is still intact. Shortly after the accident a police constable arrives at the scene and requires Billingam to provide a specimen of breath for a breath test in accordance with s. 6(2) of the Road Traffic Act 1988.

In the circumstances outlined does the constable have the power to require a specimen of breath?

A Yes, the accident does not have to be a reportable accident under s. 170 of the 1988 Act.

B No, the accident has to be a reportable accident under s. 170 of the 1988 Act.

C Yes, where the constable has reasonable cause to suspect the driver has consumed alcohol.

D No, unless the constable has reasonable cause to believe the driver is unfit through drink or drugs.

Answer RT/PS/9

A is correct.

The meaning of 'accident' in this section is not restricted to that given to a 'reportable' accident under s. 170 of the Road Traffic Act 1988.

It was held in R v Pico [1971] RTR 500 that there is no need for another vehicle in an 'accident'.

Question RT/PS/10

Clowser is involved in a road accident with another vehicle on a road. She receives minor injuries and extensive damage is caused to both her car and the other vehicle involved. The other driver calls the police from her mobile phone believing that Clowser has been drinking. Clowser provides the other driver with her name and address and then leaves the scene of the accident prior to the police arriving.

After attending the scene of the accident two police officers from your team go to Clowser's home address for the purpose of requiring a specimen of breath. She refuses them access to the property and the police officers force the front door to gain entry. They then require Clowser to provide a specimen of breath which she refuses. She is then arrested and taken to the police station.

In accordance with s. 6(2) of the Road Traffic Act 1988 – powers of entry – were the officers acting lawfully in the circumstances outlined?

A Yes, where the officers have reasonable cause to suspect an accident involving personal injury occurred they can enter, (if need be by force) any place where they suspect Clowser to be.

B No, even though an accident has occurred the officers have no power to enter the place where they suspect Clowser to be by force.

C Yes, where an accident occurred and damage was caused to a vehicle other than Clowser's vehicle.

D No, the accident must have involved injury/suspected injury to another person other than Clowser.

Answer RT/PS/10

D is correct.

Section 6(6) of the Road Traffic Act 1998 states:

(3) A constable may, for the purpose of requiring a person to provide a specimen of breath under subsection (2) above in a case where he has reasonable cause to suspect that the accident involved injury to another person or of arresting him in such a case under subsection (5) above, enter (if need be by force) any place where that person is or where the constable, with reasonable cause, suspects him to be.

Question RT/PS/11

Section 8 of the Road Traffic Act sets out the action required where an evidential specimen of breath shows no more than a certain amount of alcohol in 100 millilitres of breath.

In relation to these requirements, where two specimens of breath have been provided by a person, which of the following statements is correct?

A Where the specimen with the higher proportion of alcohol contains no more than 50 microgrammes of alcohol in 100 millilitres of breath that person may claim it should be replaced by a specimen of blood or urine.

B Where the specimen with the lower proportion of alcohol contains no more than 50 microgrammes of alcohol in 100 millilitres of breath that person may claim it should be replaced by a specimen of blood or urine.

C Where the specimen with the higher proportion of alcohol contains no more than 80 microgrammes of alcohol in 100 millilitres of breath that person has the right to provide a specimen of blood.

D. Where the specimen with the lower proportion of alcohol contains no more than 80 microgrammes of alcohol in 100 millilitres of breath that person has the right to provide a specimen of blood.

Answer RT/PS/11

B is correct.

Section 8 of the Road Traffic Act 1988 states:

(1) Subject to subsection (2) below, of any two specimens of breath provided by any person in pursuance of section 7 of this Act that with the lower proportion of alcohol in the breath shall be used and the other shall be disregarded.
(2) If the specimen with the lower proportion of alcohol contains no more than 50 microgrammes of alcohol in 100 millilitres of breath, the person who provided it may claim that it should be replaced by such specimen as may be required under section 7(4) of this Act and, if he then provides such a specimen, neither specimen of breath shall be used.

In relation to s. 7(4) the choice as to whether the person provides blood or urine will be the officer's.

Question RT/PS/12

A medical practitioner attends at your police station to obtain a blood sample from Rushton who has been arrested for drink driving. Rushton has supplied two samples of breath but the reading was such that he was given the option of providing a blood sample to which he agreed.

The doctor wishes to take the blood sample from Rushton's left arm but Rushton insists that he wants the sample taken from any other part of his body other than his arms.

Would these circumstances amount to Rushton's refusal to provide a specimen of blood?

A No, Rushton needs to consent as to which part of the body the blood will be taken from.

B Yes, it is for the doctor to say from which part of the body the blood is taken.

C No, if Rushton can show it was not his intention to obstruct the sample being obtained.

D Yes, if the doctor has reasonable cause to believe Rushton is being deliberately obstructive.

Answer RT/PS/12

B is correct.

Once consent to provide a sample is given, it is for the doctor to say from which part of the body it will be taken. Any insistence on a different course of action will be a refusal (Rushton v Higgins [1972] Crim LR 440).

Question RT/PS/13

'Post incident drinking', in relation to offences of drink driving, is dealt with by s. 15(3) of the Road Traffic Act 1988 which allows the defendant to produce evidence that the alcohol level at the time of the alleged offence was lower than shown in the analysis.

Where the process of 'back calculation' is used to determine the defendant's alcohol level at the time of the alleged offence who is permitted to introduce this in evidence?

A The court.

B The prosecution.

C The defence.

D Both the prosecution and defence.

Answer RT/PS/13

B is correct.

Section 15(2) of the Road Traffic Act 1988 limits any use of 'back calculation' to the prosecution.

In Millard v DPP (1990) 91 Cr App R 108 it was held that a defendant may not adduce back calculation evidence to show that the level of alcohol in his/her body was in fact below the amount in the specimen.

Question RT/PS/14

The police stop a vehicle that failed to comply with a lawfully placed traffic sign. The driver produces his driving licence at this time but is unable to produce a certificate of insurance. He is then required to produce a certificate of insurance for the vehicle at a nominated police station within 7 days. The driver fails to produce a certificate of insurance for the vehicle.

One of your officers, a probationer, asks you which of the following can be required by s. 171 of the Road Traffic Act 1988 to provide information as to the vehicle's policy of insurance or other acceptable form of security?

A The driver of the vehicle.

B The owner of the vehicle.

C The registered keeper of the vehicle.

D The person in charge of the vehicle.

Answer RT/PS/14

B is correct.

Section 171 of the Road Traffic Act, 1988 places a requirement on the owner of the vehicle to give such information as required by the police.

Question RT/PS/15

By virtue of s. 165 of the Road Traffic Act 1988 a person driving a motor vehicle on a road may be required by a constable or vehicle examiner to produce the relevant certificate of insurance in relation to the use of the vehicle.

This section also provides for those occasions where a person will not be convicted of failure to produce a certificate of insurance. Which of the following is NOT one of these occasions.

A Where within seven days after the date on which the production was required the certificate was produced at a police station.

B Where the certificate was produced at a police station specified by him/her as soon as was reasonably practicable.

C Where it was not reasonably practicable for the certificate to be produced there before the day on which the proceedings were commenced.

D Where the certificate was produced at the commencement of proceedings and the driver has reasonable excuse for the delay in its production.

Answer RT/PS/15

D is correct.

Section 165 of the Road Traffic Act 1988 states:

(2) A person shall not be convicted of an offence under subsection (3) above by reason only of failure to produce any certificate or other evidence . . . if in proceedings against him for the offence he shows that-
(a) within seven days after the date on which the production of the certificate or other evidence was required it was produced at a police station that was specified by him at the time when its production was required, or
(b) it was produced there as soon as was reasonably practicable, or
(c) it was not reasonably practicable for it to be produced there before the day on which the proceedings were commenced.

Question RT/PS/16

Carey, a 16 year old, is riding a motor cycle on a footpath and carrying his friend Lester, aged 15 years, as a pillion passenger. Neither Carey nor Lester are wearing motor cycle helmets.

Who, if either, commits an offence in relation to Lester not wearing protective headgear?

A Carey only.

B Lester only.

C Carey and Lester.

D Neither.

Answer RT/PS/16

C is correct.

Section 16(4) of the Road Traffic Act 1988 provides that, in relation to pillion passengers, only the person committing the offence of not wearing a helmet shall be liable unless the person is under 16. This means, that where a 16 year old rider of a motor cycle carries a 15 year old pillion passenger who is not wearing a helmet, the 16 year old will be responsible for the commission of the offence by the passenger as well as the passenger themselves.

Question RT/PS/17

By virtue of Regulation 11 of the Motorway Traffic (England and Wales) Regulations 1982, learner drivers are excluded from using motorways. However, this does not include drivers who hold ordinary licences and are learning to drive certain types of vehicles.

Which of the following is included in these types of vehicle?

A Passenger carrying vehicles.

B Armed forces vehicles.

C Heavy motor cars.

D 'Special type' vehicles.

Answer RT/PS/17

A is correct.

Learner drivers are excluded from using motorways (Regulation 11 Motorways Traffic (England and Wales) Regulations 1982), but these will not include drivers who hold ordinary licences but who are learning to drive large goods vehicles and passenger carrying vehicles.

Question RT/PS/18

Vehicles which are allowed to use motorways at any time are those falling under Class I and Class II in Schedule 4 to the Highways Act 1980.

Which of the following types of vehicles do NOT fall under Class I?

A Heavy motor cars.

B Heavy locomotives.

C Motor cycles with an engine/cylinder capacity not less than 125cc.

D Trailers being drawn by light locomotives.

Answer RT/PS/18

C is correct.

The classes of vehicles which can use motorways at any time are those falling under Class I and Class II in Schedule 4 to the Highways Act 1980. These include:
Class I
- Motor cars and motor cycles with an engine/cylinder capacity not less than 50cc
- Heavy and light locomotives and heavy motor cars
- Trailers drawn by the above

Question RT/PS/19

Following a report from a member of the public you learn that yesterday, during the hours of darkness two 19 year old youths tie a piece of rope between two trees across a footpath with the intention of causing injury to people using the footpath.

In the above circumstances did the two youths commit an offence contrary to s. 22A of the Road Traffic Act 1988 – causing danger to other road users?

A Yes, they intended to cause injury to other road users without lawful authority or reasonable excuse.

B No, a 'road' for the purpose of this offence does not include a footpath.

C Yes, it would be obvious to a reasonable person that tying the rope across the footpath would be dangerous.

D No, there was no interference with a motor vehicle, trailer or cycle.

Answer RT/PS/19

B is correct.

The Road Traffic Act 1988, s. 22A states:

(1) A person is guilty of an offence if he intentionally or without lawful authority or reasonable cause
(a) causes anything to be on or over a road, or
(b) interferes with a motor vehicle , trailer or cycle, or
(c) interferes (directly or indirectly) with traffic equipment,
in such circumstances that it would be obvious to a reasonable person that to do so would be dangerous.

A 'road' for the purpose of this offence does not include a footpath (or bridleway)
(s. 25A(5)).

Question RT/PS/20

Giles cuts the perimeter hedge round his property and lights a fire to burn the hedge cuttings. He lights the fire on his own land that runs alongside a main road. The hedge cuttings are both green and damp and this causes smoke to drift across the road. Giles' neighbour rings your police station to complain.

In relation to s. 161A of the Highways Act 1980 (dangerous activity on highways), does Giles commit an offence?

A No, the land is private and does not form part of the highway.

B Yes, he lights a fire on land not forming part of the highway and users of the highway may be endangered.

C No, unless a user of the highway was injured, interrupted or endangered.

D Yes, it would be obvious to a reasonable person that users of the highway may be injured, interrupted or endangered.

Answer RT/PS/20

C is correct.

The Highways Act 1980 s. 161A states:

(1) If a person-
(a) lights a fire on any land not forming part of a highway which consists of or comprises a carriageway; or
(b) directs or permits a fire to be lit on any such land,
and in consequence a user of any highway which consists of or comprises a carriageway is injured, interrupted or endangered by, or by smoke from, that fire or any other fire caused by that fire, that person is guilty of an offence . . .

Section 161A(1) is an offence of 'consequence', that is, it must be shown that a relevant consequence – injured, interrupted or endangered - actually occurred.

Question RT/PS/21

A local authority is dealing with a report of a motor vehicle being abandoned on a highway. In accordance with the Refuse Disposal (Amenity) Act 1978 and the Removal and Disposal of Vehicles Regulations 1986 the local authority is required to affix notices to the abandoned vehicle advising the owner of its intention.

What is the notice period required to be given by a local authority in England in relation to a vehicle that appears to have been abandoned and ought to be destroyed?

A 24 hours.

B Seven days.

C 14 days.

D 28 days.

Answer RT/PS/21

A is correct.

Before a local authority can remove a vehicle under s. 11 of the Refuse Disposal (Amenity) Act 1978, it must follow the requirements of the Act and Removal and Disposal of Vehicles Regulations 1986 in relation to affixing notices advising the owner of its intention. In order to combat the growing problem of abandoned cars, the notice period required to be given by a local authority in England in relation to a vehicle that appears to have been abandoned and ought to be destroyed is 24 hours.

Question RT/PS/22

Tonks works for a large dairy who decide, as part of their marketing strategy, to return to 'environmentally friendly' electrically powered milk floats marked up in post-war livery.

Tonks is driving his float along a public road. He has finished his deliveries and suddenly feels tired. At the side of the road is open heath and he drives 20 yards onto it and parks his vehicle to have a nap.

In these circumstances is Tonks committing an offence of driving a motor vehicle on land other than a road contrary to s.34 of the Road Traffic Act 1988.

A Yes, without lawful authority he has driven a mechanically propelled vehicle on any land, not being land forming part of a road, within 25 yards of a road for the purpose only of parking.

B No, any offence under this section relates to driving a motor vehicle, and not a mechanically propelled vehicle, onto land not being land forming part of a road.

C Yes, without lawful authority he has driven a mechanically propelled vehicle onto heath, not being land forming part of a road, over 15 yards from a road for the purpose only of parking.

D No, any offence under this section relates to driving a mechanically propelled vehicle on to or upon any common land.

Answer RT/PS/22

C is correct.

The Road Traffic Act 1988, s. 34 states:

(1) Subject to the provisions of this section, if without lawful authority a person drives a mechanically propelled vehicle-
(a) on to or upon any common land, moorland or land of any description, not being land forming part of a road, or
(b) on any road being a footpath, bridleway or restricted byway, he is guilty of an offence.

Section 34(3) provides a defence and states:
(3) It is not an offence under this section to drive a mechanically propelled vehicle on any land within fifteen yards of a road. being a road on which a motor vehicle may lawfully be driven, for the purpose only of parking the vehicle on that land.

Question RT/PS/23

Whilst on duty during the hours of darkness, you receive a complaint that a builder's skip is standing in a road. The skip is full to overflowing and there are no lights being displayed. The owner's name and telephone number are displayed on the skip and one of your officers telephones the owner requiring him to remove the skip from the highway.

Has the constable complied with the statutory requirements for requiring the removal of a skip from the highway?

A Yes, as long as the constable is in uniform and s/he speaks directly with the owner.

B No, the requirement must be made in person by the constable who must also be in uniform.

C Yes, the skip was not complying with the conditions relating to the use of the skip, i.e. not properly lit during the hours of darkness.

D No, the request must be made in person.

Answer RT/PS/23

B is correct.

Under s. 140 of the Highways Act 1980 a constable in uniform may require the removal of a skip from the highway. Failure to do so is an offence under s. 140(3) but the requirement must be made in person. If the requirement to remove the skip is made by the officer telephoning the owner, the offence will not be made out (R v Worthing Justices, ex parte Waste Management Ltd [1988] Crim LR 458).

Question RT/PS/24

Megan is driving a national blood service vehicle delivering blood as an emergency to a local hospital. She is driving through a built-up area and approaches a pelican crossing where the lights turn to red. One pedestrian is waiting at the crossing and waves Megan across. Megan then drives her vehicle over the crossing with the lights still showing a red signal. Another motorist sees the incident and reports Megan to you.

In relation to the above circumstances has Megan committed an offence contrary to s. 36 of the Road Traffic Act 1988 - failing to comply with a traffic sign?

A Yes, as a pedestrian is waiting to use the crossing, Megan must stop and accord that pedestrian precedence.

B No, she has proceeded in a manner not likely to endanger any person waiting at the crossing.

C Yes, there is no special provision for national blood service vehicles to proceed beyond the 'stop' line of a pelican crossing.

D No, national blood service vehicles are included as a special provision and pedestrians should accord precedence to them in emergencies.

Answer RT/PS/24

B is correct.

Special provision is made within regulations 12 and 13 of the Road Traffic Regulation Act 1984 in relation to vehicles being used for the purpose of:
- police
- fire brigade
- ambulance; or
- national blood service.

If a vehicle is being used for one of those purposes the driver may proceed beyond the 'stop' line if the following conditions apply:
- the driver accords precedence to any pedestrian who is on the carriageway within the limits of the crossing; and
- the driver does not proceed in a manner or at a time likely to endanger any person/vehicle approaching or waiting at the crossing; or
- the driver does not proceed in a manner or at a time likely to cause the driver of any such vehicle to change its speed or course in order to avoid an accident.

Question RT/PS/25

Barras is stopped by the police while driving his vehicle, on a road, with a defective front nearside headlamp. A constable points out the defect to Barras and he accepts a form, in accordance with the Vehicle Defect Rectification Scheme (VDRS), to have the defect remedied.

What must Barras do, in relation to the VDRS, after rectifying the defective lamp?

A Submit the vehicle for examination at a Department of Transport approved testing station for them to endorse the VDRS form after which Barras must return the form to the central police ticket office within 21 days.

B Submit the vehicle for examination by a qualified motor mechanic for them to endorse the VDRS form after which Barras must return the form to the central police ticket office within 14 days.

C Submit the vehicle for examination by a qualified motor mechanic for them to endorse the VDRS form after which Barras must return the form to the central police ticket office within 21 days.

D Submit the vehicle for examination at a Department of Transport approved testing station for them to endorse the VDRS form after which Barras must return the form to the central police ticket office within 14 days.

Answer RT/PS/25

D is correct.

The VDRS involves the person responsible being issued with a form by a police officer setting out the relevant defect in the vehicle. Once the defect has been pointed out and the person has accepted the form, they must have the defect remedied and then submit the vehicle for examination at a Department of Transport approved testing station. The testing station will certify that the defect has been rectified and the form, so endorsed, must be returned to the central police ticket office by the responsible person within 14 days.

Question RT/PS/26

You attend a fatal road traffic accident involving a family saloon car and a motor cycle. You examine the tyres of the car.

Which of the following criteria would amount to a 'defect' under the Road Vehicles (Construction and Use) in relation to the tyres?

A The tyre has a cut in excess of 25 mm or 20% of the section width of the tyre measured in any direction on the outside of the tyre and deep enough to reach the ply or cord.

B The grooves of the tread pattern of the tyre do not have a depth of at least 1 mm throughout a continuous band measuring at least three-quarters of the breadth of the tread and round the entire outer circumference of the tyre.

C The tyre has a cut in excess of 20 mm or 10% of the section width of the tyre measured in any direction on the outside of the tyre and deep enough to reach the ply or cord.

D The grooves of the tread pattern of the tyre do not have a depth of at least 1.6 mm throughout a continuous band measuring at least three-quarters of the breadth of the tread and round the entire outer circumference of the tyre.

Answer RT/PS/26

A is correct.

In the case of passenger motor cars other than cars constructed or adapted to carry more than eight passengers (in addition to the driver) the depth of tread requirement is increased to 1.6 mm throughout a continuous band across the central three-quarters section of the tyre and around the entire circumference (Road Vehicles (Construction and Use) (Amendment) (No. 4) Regulations 1990).

Question RT/PS/27

In which of the following sets of circumstances would a person NOT be committing an offence of 'quitting' contrary to Regulation 107 of the Road Vehicles (Construction and Use) Regulations 1986?

A A driver stops his motor vehicle outside a newsagent's and alights from the vehicle leaving the engine running but having set the handbrake.

B A driver stops his motor vehicle outside a newsagent's and alights from the vehicle leaving the engine running but having set the handbrake. The driver's 15 year-old brother is left in the passenger seat 'attending' the vehicle.

C A driver stops his motor vehicle outside a newsagent's and alights from the vehicle having turned off the engine but failing to set the handbrake.

D A driver stops his motor vehicle outside a newsagent's and alights from the vehicle having turned off the engine but failing to set the handbrake. The driver's brother, a lorry driver, is left in the passenger seat 'attending' the vehicle.

Answer RT/PS/27

D is correct.

Regulation 107 prohibits the leaving of a motor vehicle unattended on a road unless the engine has been stopped and the brake set; both must be done (Butterworth v Shorthouse [1956] Crim LR 341). Any person left 'attending' the vehicle must be someone who is licensed to drive it and in a position to intervene otherwise reg. 107 is breached.

Question RT/PS/28

You are on uniformed supervision duties when you see Gray driving his jeep along a public road. Travelling in the back of the uncovered jeep, which is not fitted with any restraints, is his 7 year-old son who is holding onto the vehicle's roll-bars.

Is Gray committing an offence of using a vehicle in a manner which involves danger of injury contrary to s. 40A of the Road Traffic Act 1988?

A No, the danger of injury must be to a person other than a person carried in or on that vehicle.

B Yes, but only if injury is actually sustained by any person, other than the driver, in or on that vehicle.

C No, this section only relates to the condition of a motor vehicle, the purpose for which it is being used and the number of passengers carried by it.

D Yes, the potential for injury to any person means that the offence has been committed.

Answer RT/PS/28

D is correct.

The Road Traffic Act 1988, s. 40A states:

A person is guilty of an offence if he uses, or causes or permits another to use, a motor vehicle or trailer on a road when-
(a) the condition of the motor vehicle or trailer, or of its accessories or equipment, or
(b) the purpose for which it is used, or
(c) the number of passengers carried by it, or the manner in which they are carried, or
(d) the weight, position or distribution of its load, or the manner in which it is secured,
is such that the use of the motor vehicle or trailer involves danger of injury to any person.

In a recent case a seven year-old boy was seen to be travelling in the open back of an uncovered jeep without any fitted restraints. The boy was steadying himself by holding onto the vehicle's roll-bars. The objective test as to the potential for injury meant that the offence had been committed (Gray v DPP [1999] RTR 339) under s.40A(c) due to the manner in which the 7 year old passenger was 'being carried'.

Question RT/PS/29

The day before his vehicle's test certificate expires, one of your officers, Akelis, takes his own vehicle to a drop-in Vehicle Testing Centre in his local town. The vehicle fails the test because of a defect with the silencer. Akelis drives the vehicle to a friend of his who is an automotive engineer. Five days later, after the work on the silencer has been completed, Akelis collects his vehicle to drive to the same test centre for the vehicle to be re-tested. While driving to the test centre Akelis is stopped by a constable from another police station. Akelis tells the officer about the vehicle's recent test record and where he is going. The officer tells Akelis that he is being reported for using the vehicle without a valid test certificate. Akelis asks you whether he has in fact committed any such offence in the circumstances.

Does Akelis commit an offence of using a vehicle without a current test certificate?

A Yes, where a test certificate has been refused the vehicle can only be used on a road when being driven to an authorised Vehicle Testing Centre by prior arrangement.

B No, the vehicle is being brought from a place where the relevant work has been carried out to a Vehicle Testing Centre.

C Yes, unless an authorised Vehicle Testing Centre passes the vehicle on that day.

D No, where the vehicle is being returned for testing to the same authorised Vehicle Testing Centre where the certificate was refused.

Answer RT/PS/29

B is correct.

Section 47 of the Road Traffic Act 1988 requires all motor vehicles which were first registered more than three years before the time when they are being used on a road to pass a test.

An exemption exists where the person using the vehicle is taking it to or from a testing centre. This exemption is only applicable where the test has been previously arranged with the garage. A further exemption exists where a test certificate has been refused and the vehicle is:

- being delivered by prior arrangement, or brought from the place where the relevant work is to be/has been carried out; or
- being towed to a place where it is to be broken up.

Question RT/PS/30

You are on uniformed supervision duties when you come across Stamp. Stamp was driving his vehicle along a busy main road when he had a puncture. He was unable to pull off the road at this point owing to a walled boundary running along the nearside of the road.

Stamp has placed a traffic warning triangle on the road for the purpose of warning traffic of his vehicle causing a temporary obstruction. He asks you how far must the traffic triangle be placed away from the car. Which of the following responses would be correct?

A At least 25 metres.

B At least 45 metres.

C At least 50 metres.

D At least 60 metres.

Answer RT/PS/30

B is correct.

Regulation 16 of the Traffic Signs (Temporary Obstructions) Regulations 1997 sets out a table showing the way in which various signs may be used. A sign may only be placed if the conditions specified in the table are complied with.

A traffic triangle must be placed at least 45 metres away from the obstruction.

Question RT/PS/31

Councillor Thompson is 65 years of age and recently retired from work. He is the holder of a full driving licence but is concerned about when it will need to be renewed. He is attending a local crime and disorder forum and asks for your advice

In relation to driving licences, which of the following statements is correct?

A Licences generally last until the holder's 65th birthday and are then renewable every 3 years.

B Licences generally last until the holder's 70th birthday and are then renewable every 5 years.

C Licences generally last until the holder's 65th birthday and are then renewable every 5 years.

D Licences generally last until the holder's 70th birthday and are then renewable every 3 years.

Answer RT/PS/31

D is correct.

Licences will generally last until the holder's 70th birthday or for three years, which ever is the longer. On reaching 70, a driver may renew their licence every three years.

Question RT/PS/32

As part of a high profile road safety campaign, one of your uniformed officers stops a car being driven on a road and requires the driver, Riaz, to produce her driving licence. She is unable to do so at this time.

In these circumstances does the constable now have the power to require Riaz to provide her date of birth?

A No, not unless Riaz had been the driver of a motor vehicle on a road at the time an accident occurred.

B Yes, Riaz has failed to produce her driving licence forthwith.

C No, not unless Riaz had committed an offence in relation to the use of a motor vehicle on a road.

D Yes, provided the constable suspects Riaz has not been granted a driving licence for that class of vehicle.

Answer RT/PS/32

B is correct.

The Road Traffic Act 1988, s. 164(2) states:

(2) A person required by a constable under subsection (1) above to produce his licence must in prescribed circumstances, on being so required by the constable, state his date of birth.

The 'prescribed circumstances' are set out under reg. 83 of the Motor Vehicles (Driving Licence) Regulations and include, where a person fails to produce the licence forthwith.

Question RT/PS/33

Bateman and Evans are travelling in a vehicle driven by Lynn who is a disqualified driver. Bateman believes Lynn has a provisional licence and being the holder of a full licence is supervising him as a learner driver. Evans also believes that Lynn has a provisional licence.

In relation to an offence of aiding and abetting Lynn driving whilst disqualified, who is liable?

A Bateman and Evans.

B Bateman only.

C Evans only.

D Neither.

Answer RT/PS/33

B is correct.

In relation to Bateman, where someone is supervising a 'learner driver' who turns out to be disqualified, it is reasonable to expect a supervisor to establish that the driver under their supervision has a current and valid licence.

In relation to Evans, if a passenger genuinely believes that the driver is entitled to drive the vehicle, that belief will prevent him from being charged with 'aiding and abetting' the offence under s. 103(1)(b) (Bateman v Evans (1964) 108 SJ 522).

Question RT/PS/34

At 2 pm on a Saturday afternoon a constable attends the scene of a two vehicle accident. One of the vehicles involved, driven by Pilgram, has pulled out of a junction controlled by a stop sign. After speaking with Pilgram the constable forms the opinion that she may have defective eyesight and requires her to submit to an eyesight test. The constable then picks up the registration mark which has fallen from the other vehicle in the accident and positions it on top of two cones some 20.5 metres away from where he requires Pilgram to undertake the eyesight test. She is allowed to wear spectacles after the officer has confirmed with a witness that she was wearing them at the time of the accident. You arrive at the scene.

In these circumstances has the constable complied with the requirements as to eyesight as set out in regs. 72-33 and sch. 8 of the Motor Vehicles (Driving Licences) Regulations 1999?

A Yes, as the test was properly undertaken in good light.

B No, the registration mark was not at 20 metres.

C Yes, as the test was properly undertaken in good light and the driver was permitted the aid of corrective lenses.

D No, the registration mark must be fixed to a vehicle.

Answer RT/PS/34

C is correct.

The specific requirements as to eyesight are set out at regs 762-72 and sch. 8 of the Motor Vehicles (Driving Licences) Regulations 1999. These generally require a potential driver to be able to read:

- letters and figures 79.4 mm high
- on a registration mark
- fixed to a motor vehicle
- at 20.5 metres
- in good light (with the aid of corrective lenses if worn at the time).

Question RT/PS/35

Benson and Simon both buy new Morgan sports cars. Benson has acquired a private registration mark BEN 50N and displays this on his vehicle without a space so it reads BEN50N. Simon has also acquired a private registration mark 51 MON and displays this on his vehicle in italic script so it reads *51 MON*.

In relation to the use of these registration marks who, if either, contravenes the Road Vehicles (Display of Registration Marks) Regulations 2001 which governs the form and layout of registrations marks?

A Benson and Simon

B Benson only

C Simon only

D Neither.

Answer RT/PS/35

A is correct.

Regulation 15 of the Road Vehicles (Display of Registration Marks) Regulations 2001 provides that generally characters must not be formed:

- in italic script
- using a font in which the characters are not vertical
- using multiple or broken strokes
- in such a way as to make a character(s) appear like a different character(s).

Question RT/PS/36

Guy drives a heavy goods vehicle for Spratt Haulage. The company allows Guy to take his goods vehicle home as long as it is unloaded. The journey to his home takes 30 minutes. In one week Guy drives over six consecutive days and his weekly period of driving, not including his journeys to and from Spratt Haulage, totals 54 hours.

At the end of that week Guy is involved in an accident with a police vehicle and you attend the scene.

In these circumstances has Guy exceeded the total period of driving allowed in one week by virtue of the 'drivers' hours' requirements?

A No, the journeys between his work and home are not part of his 'daily working period'.

B Yes, if the journeys between his work and home are reimbursed by the company as being part of his 'daily working period'.

C No, unless in undertaking the journeys between his work and home his goods vehicle is carrying a load.

D Yes, the journeys between his work and home are part of his 'daily working period'.

Answer RT/PS/36

D is correct.

In accordance with the Transport Act 1968 (part VI) and 'Community rules' the total period of driving in any one week must not exceed 56 hours.

In DPP v Guy [1998] RTR 82 it was held that the relevant 'daily working period' will include the time spent by a driver taking the vehicle to and from their home address before and after work.

Question RT/PS/37

Phipps, a 15 year old, visits your police station. He is making an electrically assisted pedal cycle as part of a school project. He wants to know how fast they are allowed to travel before the electric motor cuts out and how old a person needs to be to ride one. Phipps' mother is the Area Commander at your police station and has told him to come and ask you!

In relation to the Pedal Cycles (Construction and Use) Regulations 1983 and s. 32 of the Road Traffic Act 1988, what answer would you give to Phipps?

A 5 miles per hour and 12 years old or over.

B 10 miles per hour and 14 years old or over.

C 15 miles per hour and 15 years old or over.

D 20 miles per hour and 16 years old or over.

Answer RT/PS/37

B is correct.

Electrically assisted pedal cycles are cycles which do not exceed 40 kg kerbside weight (60 kg if a tandem) and which have an electric motor that is incapable of propelling the cycle once it has reached a speed of 15 miles per hour (Pedal Cycles (Construction and Use) Regulations 1983)

The only qualification or authority to ride a pedal cycle on a road is that a person must be 14 years old or over (S. 32 Road Traffic Act 1988).

INSPECTORS

Road Traffic

Question RT/I/1

During a local drink-drive campaign that you have organized in the run up to the holiday season, Watkins is arrested for an offence contrary to s. 5(1)(b) of the Road Traffic Act 1988, 'being in charge of a vehicle on a road after consuming so much alcohol that the proportion of it in his breath, blood or urine exceeds the prescribed limit.'

At the magistrates' court Watkins disputes the fact that he was 'in charge' of the vehicle at the time of his arrest. In arriving at their decision which of the following would NOT be considered by the court?

A Whether the defendant's actions were more than merely preparatory to the act of driving.

B Whether the defendant had the keys for the vehicle.

C Where the defendant was in relation to the vehicle at the time.

D What evidence there is of the defendant's intention to take control of the vehicle.

Answer RT/I/1

A is correct.

The principles to be applied when considering whether a person is 'in charge' of a vehicle are set out in DPP v Watkins [1989] 2 WLR 966. In arriving at their decision courts should consider:

- whether the defendant had the keys for the vehicle;
- where the defendant was in relation to the vehicle at the time;
- what evidence there is of the defendant's intention to take control of the vehicle.

Question RT/I/2

The defendant is driving a public service vehicle, at an excessive speed for the conditions, along a busy high street. As she approaches a pedestrian crossing, two women walk onto the crossing. The defendant inadvertently presses the accelerator pedal instead of the brake pedal and the bus accelerates and collides with the two pedestrians causing them serious injuries.

In considering an offence under s. 2A of the Road Traffic Act 1988 – dangerous driving – which of the following statements is correct?

A The fact that the defendant inadvertently pressed the accelerator may be a defence to this offence.

B This offence is specifically concerned with the manner of driving and not the defendant's state of mind.

C This offence is specifically concerned with both the defendant's state of mind and manner of driving.

D This offence is specifically concerned with a subjective test of the defendant's competence as a driver.

Answer RT/I/2

B is correct.

Section 2A(1) of the Road Traffic Act 1988 provides:

(a) the way she drives falls far below what would be expected of a competent and careful driver, and
(b) it would be obvious to a competent and careful driver that driving in that way would be dangerous.

In Attorney-General's Reference (No. 4 of 2000) [2001] RTR 415 it was held that the relevant actus reus is the act of driving in a manner which was dangerous. It was no defence to claim that the accused had not intended to press the accelerator pedal.

Question RT/I/3

In relation to an offence under s. 3 of the Road Traffic Act 1988 which of the following circumstances has it been held as insufficient evidence of driving without due care and attention?

A Evidence from the driver alone that s/he fell asleep at the wheel.

B Evidence of earlier incidents involving the driver around the same time as the offence charged.

C Evidence of expected levels of traffic, time of day and peculiar hazards.

D Evidence that the defendant departed from the required standard of driving and that his/her actions were 'voluntary'.

Answer RT/I/3

A is correct.

If a driver falls asleep at the wheel s/he will be guilty of careless driving (Henderson v Jones (1955) 119 JP 304) but evidence of this fact from the driver alone will not be enough to support a charge under s. 3 (Edwards v Clark (1951) 115 JPN 426).

Question RT/I/4

The police wish to trace the driver of a vehicle involved in a hit and run accident. Several weeks after the accident, a community officer visiting a school discovered that the accident was witnessed by two school boys who were recording vehicle registration marks as part of a geography project. The registration mark of the offending vehicle is obtained. Five days after the accident the offending driver sold the vehicle to another person who had no knowledge of the accident.

In relation to s. 172 of the Road Traffic Act 1988, to whom does the requirement to give information apply?

A The keeper of the vehicle at the time the requirement is made.

B The owner of the vehicle at the time the requirement is made.

C The keeper of the vehicle at the time of the alleged offence.

D The owner of the vehicle at the time of the alleged offence.

Answer RT/I/4

A is correct.

The requirement under s. 172 of the Road Traffic Act 1988 applies to the person keeping the vehicle and will apply to the person who is the keeper of the vehicle at the time the requirement is made even if he/she was not the keeper at the time of the alleged offence (Hateley v Greenough [1962] Crim LR 329).

Question RT/I/5

Faust drives his car, at speed, onto the gravel car park of an old factory and decides to do a handbrake turn to spin the vehicle through 180 degrees. In doing this manoeuvre he loses control of the vehicle and collides with two other cars that are unattended in the car park.

In relation to a Notice of Intended Prosecution, are the police required to serve such a Notice on Faust if they are considering taking proceedings for an offence of dangerous or careless driving?

A Yes, even where the accident occurred at the time or immediately after the offence was committed.

B No, where the offence arises from an accident that occurred on a road or public place.

C Yes, the offence arises from an accident that did not occur on a road.

D No, the accident occurred at the time or immediately after the offence was committed

Answer RT/I/5

C is correct.

Section 2(1) of the Road Traffic Offenders Act 1988 states that the requirement to serve an NIP does not apply in relation to an offence if:

- at the time or
- immediately afterwards and
- owing to the presence of the vehicle concerned
- on a road
- an accident occurs.

The exemption is limited to an accident that occurs on a road.

Question RT/I/6

Phipps is observed by a foot patrol officer overtaking on a double white line system. Later that same day he is involved in a road accident in which he receives serious injuries and is hospitalised for several weeks. The police are aware of this but a Notice of Intended Prosecution (NIP) in relation to the failure to comply with a traffic sign (double white lines) is sent by post to his home address. It is known Phipps lives alone.

In these circumstances will service by post to his home address suffice?

A Yes, the NIP can be served on him by post at his last known address.

B No, the NIP can be served on him at his last known address but only if he is discharged from hospital within 14 days of the offence.

C Yes, the NIP can be served on him at his last known address as long as an oral warning has already been given to him.

D No, the NIP can only be served by delivering it to him personally at the hospital.

Answer RT/I/6

A is correct.

If the defendant is not at his home address, for instance because he is in hospital or on holiday, service to his last known address will suffice even if the police are aware of that fact (Phipps v McCormick [1972] Crim LR 540).

Question RT/I/7

In relation to the requirements of s. 170 of the Road Traffic Act 1988 in which of the following circumstances would the driver be required to stop and give his/her name and address or report the accident to the police?

A A public service vehicle leaves the road and collides with a lamp standard. Damage is caused to the front nearside wing of the vehicle but there is no damage to the lamp standard.

B Jones is towing an agricultural trailer containing 10 live sheep that he is delivering to a new customer. He is unfamiliar with the road and misjudges the severity of a bend. He is forced to brake sharply causing the sheep to be thrown about in the trailer and one of the sheep is actually killed.

C Hosier is driving his saloon car into town when a van drives out of a junction without stopping, colliding with the nearside passenger door of Hosier's vehicle. Both vehicles sustain damage.

D Hayward is driving her new sports car along a country road when a deer runs out in front of the vehicle. She brakes sharply, missing the deer, but loses control of the car, rolling it twice, before finally coming to rest in a ditch at the side of the road.

Answer RT/I/ 7

C is correct.

Section 170 of the Road Traffic Act states:

(1) This section applies in a case where, owing to the presence of a mechanically propelled vehicle on a road or other public place, an accident occurs by which-

(a) ....

(b) damage is caused-

(i) to a vehicle other than that mechanically propelled vehicle ......

(2) The driver of the mechanically propelled vehicle must stop and, if required to do so by any person having reasonable grounds for so requiring, give his name and address ....

The section makes no mention of who may have been to blame for the accident. A driver will attract the duties imposed by s. 170 even if he/she is not at fault.

Question RT/I/8

A police patrol car is following a blue van that is being driven in excess of the speed limit and is weaving from one side of the road to the other. The police officers suspect that the driver may be unfit through drink or drugs. Before they have an opportunity to stop the vehicle it suddenly pulls into a side road and stops. The driver gets out of the vehicle and runs into a nearby house shutting the door behind him.

For the purpose of arresting a person, what powers do the officers have by virtue of s. 4 of the Road Traffic Act 1988?

A They may enter (if need be by force) any place where that person is, or where they have reasonable cause to believe he may be.

B They may enter any place where that person is or where they, with reasonable cause, suspect him to be.

C They may enter any place where that person is, or where they have reasonable cause to believe he may be.

D They may enter (if need be by force) any place where that person is, or where they, with reasonable cause, suspect him to be.

Answer RT/I/8

D is correct.

Section 4(6) and (7) of the Road Traffic Act 1988 provide that a constable may arrest without warrant if s/he has reasonable cause to suspect that the person is, or has been committing an offence under s. 4. For the purpose of arresting a person under this power, a constable may enter (if need be by force) any place where that person is or where s/he, with reasonable cause, suspects them to be.

Question RT/I/9

Denny is arrested after providing a positive specimen of breath and is taken to a nearby police station. In accordance with s. 7 of the Road Traffic Act 1988 Denny provides two specimens of breath for analysis by means of an approved device. At this point the approved device malfunctions. It is decided that Denny will be taken to your police station five miles away to provide two more specimens of breath.

In these circumstances are the officers justified in taking Denny to another police station to provide further specimens of breath?

A Yes, even if the driver has already provided two samples on an inaccurate machine they may be taken to another police station where such a machine is available.

B No, where the approved device becomes 'unavailable' for whatever reason, a blood or urine specimen must be required.

C Yes, if an approved device is 'unavailable', and with the consent of the driver, they may be taken to another police station where an approved device is 'available'.

D No, the driver can only be taken to another police station where a doctor is available to provide a blood sample.

Answer RT/I/9

A is correct.

In Denny v DPP [1990] RTR 417 it was held that the driver may be taken to another police station where an approved device is available and that this may be done even if the driver has already provided two samples on the inaccurate machine.

Question RT/I/10

A requirement under s. 7(3) of the Road Traffic Act 1988 to provide a specimen of blood cannot be made at a police station unless certain conditions apply. Which of the following is NOT one of these conditions?

A For medical reasons a specimen of breath cannot be provided or should not be required.

B The device used has not produced a reliable indication of the proportion of alcohol in the person's breath.

C Where a medical practitioner advises that the driver may be unfit due to some drug and the case involves causing death by dangerous driving.

D Where a device or reliable device used to require specimens of breath is not available at the police station.

Answer RT/I/10

C is correct.

Section 7(3) of the Road Traffic Act 1988 states:
(1) A requirement under this section to provide a specimen of blood or urine can only be made at a police station or at a hospital; and it cannot be made at a police station unless-
(a) the constable making the requirement has reasonable cause to believe that for medical reasons a specimen of breath cannot be provided or should not be required, or
(b) at the time the requirement is made a device or a reliable device of the type mentioned in subsection 1(a) above is not available at the police station or it is then for any other reason not practicable to use such a device there, or
(bb) a device of the type mentioned in subsection 1(a) above has been used at the police station but the constable who required the specimens of breath has reasonable cause to believe that the device has not produced a reliable indication of the proportion of alcohol in the breath of the person concerned, or
(c) the suspected offence is one under section 3A or 4 of this Act and the constable making the requirement has been advised by a medical practitioner that the condition of the person required to provide a specimen might be due to some drug;

The suspected offences under s. 7(3)(c) are causing death by careless driving when under the influence of drink or drugs (s. 3A) and driving or attempting to drive a mechanically propelled vehicle when unfit through drink or drugs (s. 4). Causing death by dangerous driving (s. 1) does not apply to section 7.

Question RT/I/11

In relation to drink driving s. 7(6) of the Road Traffic Act 1988 states that a person who, without reasonable excuse, fails to provide a specimen when required to do so in pursuance of this section is guilty of an offence.

Which of the following has NOT been held to be a 'reasonable excuse'?

A Mental incapacity.

B Inability to understand the requirement caused by factors other than drink or drugs.

C Inability to understand the requirement caused by self induced intoxication.

D Physical incapacity.

Answer RT/I/11

C is correct.

'Reasonable excuse' has been held to include:

Mental incapacity
Physical incapacity
Inability to understand requirement caused by factors other than drink or drugs.

Self-induced intoxication has been held not to be a reasonable excuse.

Question RT/I/12

Drummond is involved in a road accident involving two cars both of which sustain damage. She fails to stop at the scene of the accident and exchange details with the other driver. Following this she drives home and consumes a quantity of brandy. The police call at Drummond's home shortly after and require a specimen of breath that proves positive. She provides two specimens of breath at the police station and the specimen with the lower proportion of alcohol contained no more than 50 microgrammes of alcohol in 100 millilitres of breath. Drummond then provided a specimen of blood. Following the result of the analysis she is being prosecuted for driving over the prescribed limit. What is the defence allowed to show in proving that the alcohol was consumed between the time of the accident and the provision of the specimen?

A On the balance of probabilities, that the level of alcohol in the defendant's body at the time of the accident was lower than that at the time of the analysis.

B Beyond a reasonable doubt, that the level of alcohol in the defendant's body at the time of the accident was lower than that at the time of the analysis.

C By using a method of 'back calculation', that the level of alcohol in the defendant's body at the time of the accident was lower than that at the time of the analysis.

D There is reasonable cause to believe that the level of alcohol in the defendant's body at the time of the accident was lower than that at the time of the analysis.

Answer RT/I/12

A is correct.

Section 15(3) of the Road Traffic Act 1988 allows the defence to show, on the balance of probabilities, that the level of alcohol in the defendant's body at the time of the alleged offence was lower than that at the time of the analysis.

In Millard v DPP (1990) 91 Cr App R 108 it was held that a defendant may not adduce back calculation evidence to show that the level of alcohol in his/her body was in fact below the amount in the specimen.

Question RT/I/13

After an accident Webber, one of the drivers involved, is taken to hospital for treatment. At the hospital she is required to provide a specimen of breath under s.6 of the Road Traffic Act 1988, she refused. While still a patient at the hospital Webber is required to provide a blood specimen. She agreed but, before she was able to provide the specimen, she was discharged. She was then arrested as a result of her earlier refusal and taken to your police station where a blood specimen is obtained.

Webber complains to you that the procedure followed was unlawful.

In relation to the above circumstances, where should the blood specimen have been taken from Webber?

A Because the request was made while Webber was a patient at the hospital, the blood specimen should have been taken at the hospital.

B Had Webber been arrested at the hospital when she refused to provide a specimen of breath, the blood specimen should have been taken at the hospital.

C Because the blood specimen was not taken from Webber at the hospital before her discharge, following her discharge she should have again been required to provide a blood specimen which could have been taken at the police station.

D Once an obligation to provide a specimen for analysis has been made it is irrelevant where the specimen is actually taken.

Answer RT/I/13

D is correct.

In Webber v DPP [1998] RTR 111 the driver of a vehicle involved in an accident was taken to a hospital where she was requested to provide a specimen of breath under s. 6. She refused. While she was still a patient at the hospital, the driver was required to provide a blood specimen for analysis under ss. 7(1)(b) and 9(1). She agreed but, before she was able to provide the specimen, she was discharged. She was then arrested under s. 6(5)(b) as a result of her earlier refusal. The driver was taken to a police station where she provided a specimen of blood. Webber was subsequently convicted of driving over the prescribed limit. She appealed on the ground that s. 9(1)(a) required the blood specimen to be taken at the hospital, which in this case it was not. It was held that, once the obligation to provide a specimen for analysis has been made, it is not to be discharged simply by an 'irrelevant change of focus'.

Question RT/I/14

The risks which must generally be covered by any insurance policy for the purposes of s. 143 of the Road Traffic Act 1988 are set out in s. 143(5). Which of the following is NOT one of these risks?

A Liability in relation to bodily injury caused to others when the vehicle is on a road in Great Britain.

B Civil liability in relation to the use of a vehicle from another EU member state in Great Britain.

C Liability in relation to damage caused to other vehicles when the vehicle is on a road in Great Britain

D Civil liability in relation to the use of a vehicle from Great Britain in another EU member state.

Answer RT/I/14

C is correct.

The risks that must be covered by any insurance policy for the purposes of s. 143 are set out in s. 143(5). These are generally:

- Liability in relation to bodily injury caused to others when the vehicle is on a road in Great Britain.
- Civil liability in relation to the use of a vehicle from another EU member state in Great Britain.
- Civil liability in relation to the use of a vehicle from Great Britain in another EU member state.

Question RT/I/15

Khan is driving his two-seater sports car on a road and is carrying three passengers who are crammed in and behind the passenger seat. He is involved in an accident with another vehicle with damage being caused to both vehicles. On being required by the police, Khan produces a certificate of insurance for the date of the accident. However, the policy has a restriction written into it that the vehicle should not carry more than one other person in addition to the driver.

Your desk officer asks you whether, in relation to the above circumstances, there is a certificate of insurance in force in relation to the use of the vehicle at the time of the accident for the purposes of s. 143 of the Road Traffic Act 1988. Is there?

A No, this restriction is not excluded by virtue of s. 148(1) of the 1988 Act.

B Yes, this restriction is excluded by virtue of s. 148(1) of the 1988 Act.

C No, the restrictions excluded by virtue of s. 148(1) of the 1988 Act only relate to the driver or physical characteristics of the vehicle.

D Yes, this restriction is excluded by virtue of s. 148(1) of the 1988 Act but only where the vehicle is being used for a purpose covered by the policy of insurance.

Answer RT/I/15

B is correct.

Section 148(1) of the Road Traffic Act 1988 makes the effects of some restrictions in a policy void in relation to s. 143. This means that, if a policy purports to restrict the extent of its cover by reference to any of these features, breach of them by the insured person will not affect the validity of that policy for the purposes of s. 143. The features under s. 148 include:

(1) . . .

(a) the age or physical or mental condition of persons driving the vehicle,

(b) the condition of the vehicle,

(c) the number of persons that the vehicle carries,

(d) . . .

Question RT/I/16

In relation to Schedule 2 to the Motor Vehicles (Wearing of Seat Belts) Regulations 1993 on which of the following occasions will it be deemed that a seat belt is NOT 'available'?

A The seat is properly occupied by someone wearing the seat belt.

B The seat is being used for a carry cot containing a child under one year old which cannot go anywhere else in the vehicle.

C The seat is occupied by someone with a medical exemption.

D The seat is occupied by a child under the age of 14 years and less than 150 centimetres in height.

Answer RT/I/16

D is correct.

Schedule 2 to the Motor Vehicles (Wearing of Seat Belts) Regulations 1993 expands on a number of occasions where seat belts will be deemed not to be 'available'. These occasions include:

- where the seat is properly occupied by someone wearing the seat belt;
- where the seat is being used for a carry cot containing a child under one year old which cannot go anywhere else in the vehicle.
- where the seat is occupied by someone with a medical exemption.

Question RT/I/17

In relation to offences of exceeding the speed limit, which of the following statements is incorrect?

A A person shall not be convicted solely on the evidence of one witness to the effect that, in his/her opinion, the defendant was exceeding the speed limit.

B Where two police officers provide sufficient evidence of a vehicle's speed it is important to show that both officers saw the vehicle at exactly the same time.

C Where corroboration is provided by VASCAR, or similar speed measuring equipment, it is necessary to prove the accuracy of the equipment being used.

D The requirements for corroboration do not apply to general speeding offences on motorways.

Answer RT/I/17

C is correct.

Corroboration may be provided by the equipment in a police vehicle or by Vascar or similar speed measuring equipment (Nicholas v Penny [1950] 2 All ER 89). While it may be preferable it is not necessary in such cases to prove the accuracy of the equipment being used (see e.g. Darby v DPP [1995] RTR 294).

Question RT/I/18

You are approached by a group of residents from a housing estate who are concerned about side roads on their estate being used to commit crime and evade arrest. The residents have heard something about a new Countryside and Rights of Way Act that allows local highway authorities to make a special order to stop up or divert a highway where specific conditions are met.

Which of the following conditions must be met whereby a local highway authority is empowered to stop up or divert a highway under the Highways Act 1980 (as amended by the Countryside and Rights of Way Act 2000)?

A Where they are satisfied that premises adjoining or adjacent to the highway are affected by high levels of crime and that the existence of the highway is facilitating the persistent commission of criminal offences.

B Where there is reasonable cause to believe that premises adjoining or adjacent to the highway are affected by high levels of crime and anti-social behaviour to the annoyance of residents and users of the highway.

C Where they are satisfied that premises adjoining or adjacent to the land are affected by high levels of crime and that the existence of the highway is facilitating the persistent commission of criminal offences.

D Where there is reasonable cause to believe that land adjoining or adjacent to the highway is affected by high levels of crime and anti-social behaviour to the annoyance of residents and users of the highway.

Answer RT/I/18

A is correct.

The Highways Act 1980 has been amended by the Countryside and Rights of Way Act 2000, to allow local highway authorities to stop up or divert highways where it is expedient to do so for the purposes of preventing or reducing crime which would otherwise disrupt the life of the community. The local highway authority can make a special order, either stopping or diverting the relevant highway, where they are satisfied that premises adjoining or adjacent to the highway are affected by high levels of crime and that the existence of the highway is facilitating the persistent commission of criminal offences.

Question RT/I/19

The Terrorism Act 2000 empowers any officer of or above the rank of Assistant Chief Constable/Commander, in order to prevent acts of terrorism, to authorise the use of stop and search powers and impose prohibitions or restrictions on parking in a specified area for a certain period of time.

What is the maximum period of time where such an authority can be used?

A A period not exceeding seven days.

B A period not exceeding 14 days.

C A period not exceeding 21 days.

D A period not exceeding 28 days.

Answer RT/I/19

D is correct.

Where it appears to any officer of or above the rank of Assistant Chief Constable/Commander that it is expedient to do so, in order to prevent acts of terrorism, he/she may authorise the use of stop and search powers in a locality for a period not exceeding 28 days (ss. 44 and 46 of the Terrorism Act 2000) and to impose prohibitions or restrictions on parking in a specified area (s.48).

Question RT/I/20

The Road Traffic Act, s. 19(1) makes it an offence to park a heavy commercial vehicle wholly or partly on the verge of a road, or on any land situated between two carriageways and which is not a footway, or on a footway.
In relation to the above offence, s.19(2) provides for a defence. Which of the following is NOT a defence as contained within this subsection?

A That the vehicle was parked in accordance with permission given by a constable or traffic warden.

B That the vehicle was parked in accordance with permission given by a constable in uniform.

C That the vehicle was parked in contravention of this section for the purpose of saving life.

D That the vehicle was parked in contravention of this section for the purpose of extinguishing fire.

Answer RT/I/20

A is correct.

The Road Traffic Act 1988 s. 19(2) states:

(2) A person shall not be convicted of an offence under this section in respect of a vehicle if he proves to the satisfaction of the court-
(a) that it was parked in accordance with permission given by a constable in uniform, or
(b) that it was parked in contravention of this section for the purpose of saving life or extinguishing fire or meeting any other like emergency, . . .

Question RT/I/21

A constable is on patrol when he finds a stationary and unattended vehicle parked near the brow of a hill on a busy main road. This part of the road is controlled by a double white line system. Immediate enquiries are made of the registered keeper of the vehicle who states she sold the vehicle several weeks previously but cannot remember to whom she sold it.

Under what circumstances does the constable have the power to remove the vehicle (under the Removal and Disposal of Vehicles Regulations 1986)?

A If it has broken down in such a position as to cause obstruction to persons using the road.

B If it has been permitted to remain at rest on a road in contravention of a prohibition or restriction contained in the Regulations.

C If s/he arranges for a reputable contractor to remove the vehicle and chooses that contractor with reasonable care.

D If it appears to be broken down on a road and to have been abandoned without lawful authority.

Answer RT/I/21

B is correct.

Regulation 3 of the Removal and Disposal of Vehicles Regulations 1986 – police powers to remove vehicles from roads - 1986 applies to vehicles which:

- have broken down, or permitted to remain at rest, on a road in such a position or in such condition or in such circumstances as to cause obstruction to persons using the road or as to be likely to cause danger to such persons, or
- have been permitted to remain at rest or have broken down and remained at rest on a road in contravention of a prohibition or restriction contained in it, or having effect under, any of the enactments mentioned in sch. 1 to these Regulations.

Regulation 4 of the 1986 Regulations states:

Where a vehicle-

(a) is a vehicle to which Regulation 3 of these Regulations applies, or

(b) . . .

(c) . . .

then, subject to the provisions of sections 99 and 100 of the Road Traffic Regulations Act 1984, a constable may remove or arrange for the removal of the vehicle …'

Section 99 of the Road Traffic Regulations Act 1984 provides for the removal of vehicles illegally parked.

Question RT/I/22

Permission to deposit a builder's skip on a highway is given by the highway authority. Such permission may be either unconditional or subject to such conditions as may be specified. However, s. 139 of the Highways Act 1980 places certain standard requirements on the owner of the skip irrespective of any other specific conditions that the highway authority may impose.

Which below is NOT one of these standard requirements contained in s. 139?

A That the skip is properly lighted during the hours of darkness.

B That the skip is clearly and indelibly marked with the owner's name and with his telephone number or address.

C That the skip is removed as soon as practicable after it has been filled.

D That the skip may not be sited on driveways.

Answer RT/I/22

D is correct.

The Highways Act 1980, s. 139 states:

(1) A builder's skip shall not be deposited on a highway without the permission of the highway authority for the highway.

(2) A permission under this section shall be a permission for a person to whom it is granted to deposit, or cause to be deposited, a skip on the highway specified in the permission, and a highway authority may grant such permission either conditionally or subject to such conditions as may be specified in the permission, including, in particular, conditions relating to-

(a) the siting of the skip;

(b) its dimensions;

(c) the manner in which it is to be coated with paint and other material for the purpose of making it immediately visible to oncoming traffic;

(d) the care and disposal of its contents;

(e) the manner in which it is to be lighted or guarded;

(f) its removal at the end of the period of permission.

(3) . . .

(4) Where a builder's skip has been deposited on a highway in accordance with a permission granted under this section, the owner of the skip shall secure-

(a) that the skip is properly lighted during the hours of darkness...;

(b) that the skip is clearly and indelibly marked with the owner's name and with his telephone number and address;

(c) that the skip is removed as soon as practicable after it has been filled;

Question RT/I/23

A local primary school is holding a parents' open evening in June starting at 6.30pm. The road outside the school is usually busy with traffic up until 7pm and the Head Teacher of the school wants to ask the school crossing patrol to assist parents across the road between 6pm and 6.30pm but is not sure if this would be permitted. The Head Teacher wants your advice.

In relation to the above circumstances, and the provisions for school crossing patrols, which of the following statements is correct?

A They can only operate between 8.00 am and 5.30 pm.

B They only have the power to stop vehicles for adults unless children are crossing at the same time.

C They can be operated at any time and can allow anyone to cross safely.

D They can be operated at any time where the authority of the relevant Head Teacher has been obtained.

Answer RT/I/23

C is correct.

The Transport Act 2000 removed the restrictions on the times of day when a school crossing patrol could be operated. Also the restriction on only stopping traffic when children are crossing has been removed to enable patrols to stop traffic in order to allow anyone to cross safely.

Question RT/I/24

In relation to using a motor vehicle with a defective tyre, Regulation 27(4) of the Road Vehicles (Construction and Use) 1986 sets out a number of exemptions to some of the provisions.

Which of the following is such an exemption?

A Broken down vehicles being drawn by a motor vehicle at not more than 30 miles per hour.

B Agricultural motor vehicles being driven at not more than 25 miles per hour.

C Vehicles proceeding to a place to be broken up driven at not more than 15 miles per hour.

D Agricultural trailers.

Answer RT/I/24

D is correct.

Regulation 27(4) of the Road Vehicles (Construction and Use) Regulations 1986 sets out a number of exemptions to the provisions contained in subsection 1(a) – (g), the main ones being:

- agricultural motor vehicles driven at no more than 20 mph
- agricultural trailers
- broken down vehicles or vehicles proceeding to a place to be broken up, being drawn in either case, by a motor vehicle at no more than 20 mph.

Question RT/I/25

Where a person is in breach of the relevant weight requirement for a goods or passenger vehicle contrary to s. 41B(1) of the Road Traffic Act 1988, subsection (2) provides for a statutory defence.

Which of the following would be such a defence?

A That, for the purpose of being weighed, the vehicle was proceeding to a weighbridge which was nearest to where the loading had been completed.

B That after being weighed the vehicle was proceeding to where it had been loaded in order to reduce the weight to the relevant limit.

C Where the limit of that weight was not exceeded by 5% and that limit was not exceeded at the time the vehicle was loaded.

D Where the limit of that weight was not exceeded by 5% and that since the time loading had been completed no person had made any addition to the load.

Answer RT/I/25

A is correct.

The Road Traffic Act 1988, s. 41B states:

(2) In any proceedings for an offence under this section, in which there is alleged a contravention of or failure to comply with a construction and use requirement as to any description of weight applicable to a goods vehicle, it shall be a defence to prove either-

(a) that at the time when the vehicle was being used on the road-

(i) it was proceeding to a weighbridge which was the nearest available one to the place where the loading of the vehicle was completed for the purpose of being weighed, or

(ii) it was proceeding from a weighbridge after being weighed to the nearest points at which it was reasonably practicable to reduce the weight to the relevant limit, without causing an obstruction on any road, or

(b) in a case where the limit of that weight was not exceeded by more than 5 per cent-

(i) that the limit was not exceeded at the time when the loading of the vehicle was originally completed, and

(ii) that since that time no person has made any addition to the load.

Question RT/I/26

Police Officers in uniform and other authorised vehicle examiners have the power to test any vehicle on any premises where that vehicle is located in accordance with certain provisions contained in Regulation 74 of the Road Vehicles (Construction and Use) Regulations 1986.

Which of the following conditions is NOT a requirement before such a test or inspection can be carried out?

A The owner of the vehicle consents.

B Personal notice has been given to the owner of the vehicle not less than 48 hours before the time of the proposed test/inspection.

C The test or inspection is made within 72 hours of a reportable accident in which the vehicle was involved.

D Notice has been sent to the owner by recorded delivery at least 72 hours before the proposed test/inspection.

Answer RT/I/26

C is correct.

Regulation 74 of the Road Vehicles (Construction and Use) Regulations 1986 provides that no test or inspection shall be carried out unless:

- the owner of the vehicle consents;
- notice has been given to that owner (either personally or left at his/her address not less than 48 hours before the time of the proposed test/inspection, or sent to him/her by recorded delivery at least 72 hours before the proposed test/inspection; or
- the test or inspection is made within 48 hours of a reportable accident in which the vehicle was involved.

Question RT/I/27

Your police station receives a request from a cycling club about their annual road-racing event taking place over a two-week period in August. The request identifies certain areas of road that the club consider dangerous owing to parked vehicles and asks if your officers can place 'No Waiting' signs at these danger spots for the duration of the event, like they did last year.

Section 67 of the Road Traffic Regulation Act 1984 provides that a constable may place on a road, traffic signs indicating prohibitions, restrictions or requirements relating to vehicular traffic to prevent danger to or from traffic in such circumstances.

For how long a period can the signs be maintained? A period of:

A 24 hours or less.

B 72 hours or less.

C Seven days or less.

D 14 days or less.

Answer RT/I/27

C is correct.

The Road Traffic Regulation Act 1984, s. 67 states:

(1) A constable, or a person acting under the instructions (whether general or specific) of the chief officer of police, may place on a road, or on any structure on a road, traffic signs (of any size, colour and type prescribed or authorised under section 64 of this Act) indicating prohibitions, restrictions or requirements relating to vehicular traffic, as may be necessary or expedient to prevent or mitigate congestion or obstruction of traffic, or danger to or from traffic, in consequence of extraordinary circumstances; and the power to place signs conferred by the subsection shall include power to maintain a sign for a period of seven days or less from the time when it was placed, but no longer.

Question RT/I/28

A traffic survey is being conducted on a main road using a lay-by to undertake the survey. A constable employed to direct traffic into the census area directs a motor vehicle being driven by Kira into the lay-by. Kira stops her vehicle and tells the constable she is late for an appointment and does not wish to provide information for the survey. She then drives off without waiting for any further direction.

In these circumstances does Kira commit an offence contrary to s. 35 of the Road Traffic Act 1988 – failing to comply with the directions of a constable?

A No, unnecessary delay must not be caused to someone who is unwilling to provide information for the purpose of the survey.

B Yes, the constable has the power to direct traffic into a census area for the purpose of a traffic survey and drivers must comply.

C No, provided the driver has stopped in compliance with the constable's direction and the purpose is other than the commission of an offence.

D Yes, the driver is required to stop at a traffic survey for the purpose of relevant questions being put to them.

Answer RT/I/28

A is correct.

The Road Traffic Act 1988, s. 35(2) provides a police power to direct traffic into a census area for the purpose of a traffic survey. Section 35(3) states that the power must not be used in such a way as to cause unnecessary delay to someone who indicates that they are unwilling to provide information for the purposes of the survey

Question RT/I/29

A traffic warden is regulating traffic when a pedestrian, Clark, walks across the carriageway in contravention of the traffic warden's direction for pedestrians to stop. The traffic warden requires Clark to give her name and address but she refuses. Clark is an off duty police officer and a complaint is made to you about the incident.

Does Clark commit an offence of failing to provide her name and address in accordance with s. 169 of the Road Traffic Act 1988?

A No, the requirement can only be made by a constable.

B Yes, the requirement can be made by a constable or traffic warden.

C No, the requirement by a traffic warden can only be made of a person driving a vehicle on a road.

D Yes, the requirement can be made by a traffic warden under the direction of a constable.

Answer RT/I/29

B is correct.

The Road Traffic Act 1988, s. 37 provides that where a constable (or traffic warden) is engaged in the regulation of vehicular traffic in a road, a person on foot who proceeds across or along the carriageway in contravention of a direction to stop, either to persons on foot or to persons on foot and other traffic, is guilty of an offence.

Section 169 of the Act requires that a person committing an offence under s. 37 to give his/her name and address to the constable (or traffic warden).

Question RT/I/30

Mooney has been arrested and charged with driving a motor vehicle while disqualified. When Mooney appears at court the prosecution are required to 'prove' she was disqualified.

Which of the following is NOT an accepted way of 'proving' such disqualification?

A On Mooney's own admission that she was disqualified in interview under caution.

B By the evidence of someone who was present in court at the time Mooney was disqualified.

C On Mooney's own admission that she was disqualified in evidence before the court.

D By the evidence of a constable who was the officer in the case which led to Mooney's disqualification.

Answer RT/I/30

D is correct.

The ways in which a driver's disqualification can be 'proved' are:

- By a certificate under s. 73(4) of the Police and Criminal Evidence Act 1984
- By the evidence of someone who was present in court at the time the person was disqualified (R v Derwentside Justices, ex parte Heaviside [1996] RTR 384)
- On the defendant's own admission, both in interview under caution and in evidence before the court (Moran v CPS (2000) 164 JP 562 and DPP v Mooney [1997] RTR 434.

Question RT/I/31

Courts have a power to impose interim disqualification from driving under certain conditions on a defendant who has been convicted of a relevant offence.

In which of the following conditions will this power NOT be available?

A Where the defendant is committed to the Crown Court for trial.

B Where passing sentence on the defendant is deferred.

C Where the defendant is committed to the Crown Court for sentence.

D Where the defendant is remitted to another magistrates' court.

Answer RT/I/31

A is correct.

Courts have the power to impose an interim disqualification under certain conditions:
- a magistrates' court committing a person to the Crown Court for sentence
- remitting the person to another magistrates' court
- deferring passing sentence on a person
- adjourning after convicting a person but before dealing with them for the offence.

A magistrates' court cannot impose an interim disqualification when committing a defendant for trial.

Question RT/I/32

Regulation 17 of the Motor Vehicles (Driving Licences) Regulations 1999 place certain requirements on a person supervising a learner driver who must be a 'qualified driver'.

In relation to this regulation, which of the following statements contains the correct criteria for a 'qualified driver,?

A A person 21 years of age or over, holding a relevant licence, and has held a relevant full licence for a continuous period of not less than three years.

B A person 21 years of age or over, holding a relevant licence, and has held a relevant full licence for a continuous or aggregate period of three years.

C A person 21 years of age or over, holding a relevant licence, and has held a relevant full licence for a continuous period of four years.

D A person 21 years of age or over, holding a relevant licence, and has held a relevant full licence for a continuous or aggregate period of four years.

AnswerRT/I/32

A is correct.

Regulation 17 of the Motor Vehicles (Driving Licences) Regulations 1999 states:

(1) subject to paragraph (2), a person is a qualified driver for the purpose of regulation 16 if he-
(a) is 21 years of age or over,
(b) holds a relevant licence,
(c) has the relevant driving experience,
(d) . . .

'Relevant driving experience' is defined at reg. 17(3)(d) as a person who has held the relevant full licence for a continuous period of not less than three years.

Question RT/I/33

Nicole passed her driving test in her Renault Clio. Nine months after passing her test she receives a Fixed Penalty Notice for speeding which she pays and has three penalty points endorsed on her licence. 6 months later she is again caught speeding and receives a further three points on her licence.

In relation to the Road Traffic (New Drivers) Act 1995, will Nicole lose her entitlement to drive?

A Yes, the probationary period for a new driver is two years and Nicole has accumulated six penalty points.

B No, the probationary period for a new driver is one year.

C Yes, the probationary period for a new driver is 18 months and Nicole has received six penalty points.

D No, the probationary period for a new driver is for two years but the driver must have accumulated over six penalty points.

Answer RT/I/33

A is correct.

The Road Traffic (New Drivers) Act 1995 set out a 'probationary' period of two years and if, during that period, a driver received six or more penalty points on his/her licence, the full entitlement to drive will be lost (s. 2).

Question RT/I/34

Under regulation 4 of the Vehicle Excise Duty (Immobilisation, Removal and Disposal of Vehicles) Regulations 1997, certain unlicensed vehicles are generally exempt from being clamped while stationary on a public road.

Which of the following vehicles is NOT generally exempt under this regulation?

A Vehicles that appear to have been abandoned.

B Vehicles displaying a current disabled person's badge.

C Vehicles stationary at a time when less than 24 hours have elapsed since their release from immobilization/removal.

D Vehicles exempt from excise duty and displaying nil licences.

Answer RT/I/34

D is correct.

Under reg. 4 the vehicles generally exempt from the provisions of the 1997 Regulations when being used on a public road are:
- Vehicles displaying a disabled person's badge
- Vehicles stationary at a time within 24 hours from their release from immobilization/removal
- Vehicles that appear to have been abandoned
- Vehicles displaying a British Medical Association badge
- PSV's, and vehicles being public utility or the post office
- Vehicles exempt from excise duty and displaying nil licences

Question RT/I/35

A constable visits a garage owned by Crimmins which is used for the sale of new and used motor vehicles. The constable notices that on one of the vehicles at the back of the garage there is what appears to be a trade plate fastened to the front grill of the vehicle. On closer inspection the constable finds that the 'trade plate' is not an authorised plate. Crimmins admits he made the plate saying he has applied for a trade licence but has not yet received it.

In these circumstances does Crimmins commit an offence of displaying a plate which could be mistaken as a trade plate contrary to reg. 32 of the Road Vehicles (Registration and Licensing) Regulations 1971?

A No, the vehicle must be on a public road.

B Yes, the vehicle does not have to be on a public road.

C No, provided he has made application for a trade licence and is using the plate in the course of his business.

D Yes, if Crimmins' intent to use the vehicle on a public road can be proved.

Answer RT/I/35

B is correct

Regulation 32(1) of the Road Vehicles (Registration and Licensing) Regulations 1971, provide that it is an offence to exhibit:

- a trade plate that has been altered or defaced,
- a trade plate that is illegible, or
- anything that could be mistaken for a trade plate

on a mechanically propelled vehicle.

Reg. 32(2) does not specify that the vehicle must be on a public road.

Question RT/I/36

Under the Transport Act, 1968, s. 99(1), in relation to the use of goods and passenger vehicles, a constable may require any person to produce and permit for inspection and copy any record sheet, book, register or document required to be carried on the vehicle or preserved. If a person required to produce the record sheet, etc., is unable to do so at the time, provision is made for their production at a later date.

In regard to the production of any such record etc. at a later date, which of the following statements is correct?

A A notice must be served on the person for their production at a police station specified not less than seven days from the service of the notice.

B A notice must be served on the person for their production at the office of the traffic commissioner specified not less than seven days from the service of the notice.

C A notice must be served on the person for their production at a police station specified not less than 10 days from the service of the notice.

D A notice must be served on the person for their production at the office of the traffic commissioner specified not less than 10 days from the service of the notice.

Answer RT/I/36

D is correct.

The Transport Act 1968, s. 99 provides that any record sheet, book, register or document shall, if the officer so requires by notice in writing served on that person, be produced at the office of the traffic commissioner specified not less than 10 days from the service of the notice.

Question RT/I/37

Olson has made an application to his local authority for a taxi drivers' licence. He has recently been acquitted at the Crown Court for an offence of assault with intent to rob but you wish to oppose the granting of his licence.

Which of the following statements is correct?

A Olson need only satisfy the granting authority that he is a fit and proper person.

B The granting authority may decide against the application on the civil law standard of 'a balance of probabilities'.

C The granting authority cannot take account of Olson's recent acquittal when applying the civil law standard.

D The granting authority may only decide against the application on the criminal law standard of 'beyond reasonable doubt'.

Answer RT/I/37

B is correct

An application for a taxi drivers' licence must satisfy the granting authority that s/he is a fit and proper person. The authority may decide against the application on the civil law standard of a 'balance of probabilities', even where it is considering the applicant's acquittal for a criminal offence (R v Maidstone Crown Court, ex parte Olson (1992) The Times, 21 May).

Question RTR/I/38

Garbutt is given a fixed penalty ticket for a non-endorsable offence. By the end of the suspended enforcement period Garbutt has not paid the fixed penalty, or given notice requesting a court hearing.

Which of the following sum may the police register for enforcement against Garbutt?

A A sum equal to 1.25 times the amount of the penalty.

B A sum equal to 1.5 times the amount of the penalty.

C A sum equal to 1.75 times the amount of the penalty.

D A sum equal to twice the amount of the penalty.

Answer RT/I/38

B is correct

The Road Traffic Offenders Act 1988, s.62 provides that where the driver of a vehicle is not present and a fixed penalty notice is fixed to the vehicle if the penalty has not been paid by the end of the suspended enforcement period, the police may serve a 'notice to owner' on the person who appears to be the owner of the vehicle. If there is no response to the 'notice to owner' the police may register a sum equal to 1.5 times the amount of the penalty for enforcement against that person. Where this happens, the justices' clerk for the area where the person lives will notify the person to that effect.

The recipient can then make a statutory declaration (under sch. 4) to the effect that:

- S/he did not know of the fixed penalty notice until he received notification from the clerk
- S/he was not the owner of the vehicle at the time
- S/he gave notice requesting a court hearing

Question RT/I/39

Palmer is riding his pedal cycle when he fails to stop at a 'give way' sign and collides with a police patrol car on a main road causing damage to both the car and pedal cycle. Palmer provides his name and address to the driver of the police vehicle but the officer's supervisor later tells him to go and test Palmer's brakes. The officer questions whether he is empowered to do this and a disagreement develops.

In relation to testing the braking system of Palmer's pedal cycle (in accordance with regulation 11 of the Pedal Cycles (Construction and Use) Regulations 1983), when may the officer carry out such a test?

A Within 48 hours on any premises without the consent of the owner of the premises.

B Within 48 hours on any premises with the consent of the owner of the premises.

C Within 72 hours on any premises without the consent of the owner of the premises.

D Within 48 hours on any premises with the consent of the owner of the cycle.

Answer RT/I/39

B is correct.

Regulation 11 of the Pedal Cycles (construction and Use) Regulations 1983 provides that a constable in uniform may test a pedal cycle to ensure conformity with the braking system requirements:

- on a road
- if the cycle has been involved in a road accident within 48 hours before the test, on any premises provided the owner of the premises consents.

FREE Trial
MCQ Interactive CD-ROM

MCQ Interactive, the computerised question and answer programme, is easy to use, even for complete computer novices, and it contains the full range of MCQs which can be infinitely regenerated. You can also prepare your own MCQs with MCQ Designer.

To claim your FREE Trial copy of the MCQ Interactive CD-ROM complete this order form below and attach one token from each of the other three MCQ Books on the reverse of this page. You need only complete one order form.

Return the order form (FREEPOST) to:

Detail Technologies Limited, FREEPOST
PO Box 43, Porth, CF39 8WR.

Name:

Rank:

Address:

County: Postcode:

Daytime Telephone No:

Email Address:

Mobile Tel. No:

Mobile Provider:

Police Force:

☐ Tick this box if you do not want us to send you information on other related products and offers.

FREE Trial
MCQ Interactive CD-ROM

Attach your three tokens from the other MCQ Books in the spaces provided below. Complete the order form overleaf and return to **Detail Technologies Limited, FREEPOST PO Box 43, Porth, CF39 8WR.**